Champions of Character

**A TRUE STORY ABOUT GRIT...
AND A SMALL-TOWN BASKETBALL TEAM**

By Mary Fichtner
Photographs by Julie Taylor

This book is dedicated to the Burns Broncs Boys' Basketball Seniors of 2015; Rowan, Noah, Tyler, Cole, Carter, Dylan, Matt, and Craig.

You changed many hearts and lives with your deeds and this story is to honor you! You didn't know how your story would end but you chose to try and change your stars. I am so thankful to have been there for every play!

Tyler, We all miss you every day!

Champions of Character: A True Story About Grit… and a Small-Town Basketball Team

© 2022 by Mary Fichtner
All rights reserved

No part of this book may be reproduced in any form or by any means, electronic or mechanical including photocopy, information storage or a retrieval system without the express and written consent of the author. Reproductions of the cover or brief quotations from the text are permitted when used in conjunction with book reviews by qualified editors or authors.

Photography by Julie Taylor

Layout and Design by Andy Grachuk
www.JingotheCat.com

Cole, Rowan, Tyler, Dylan, Noah, Craig, Carter (Matt not pictured)

"A thatcher's son? A knight? You might as well try to change the stars."

"Can it be done? Can a man change his stars?"

"Yes, if he believes enough, a man can do anything!"

(an excerpt from A Knight's Tale)

"Hardships often prepare ordinary people for an extraordinary destiny."

CS Lewis, writer, and theologian.

The Season

Burns, Wyoming is a typical water tower town; one where people live spread out but community is strong. Like most small towns, folks gather at High School sporting events. The fans talk, predict and speculate about each team and every sport in advance; basketball is a particular favorite. Every year the high school gym becomes the hotspot of intriguing stories and memories to last a lifetime.

The team of 2015's story is one that won't be forgotten; life lessons for those who choose to take note. It is the true story of an underdog; a small-town team with nothing but a longshot. It's a story only those who witnessed would believe. That is why it was a season to remember.

The Stars

There is always the expectation that the upcoming team would spend a lot of their summer playing basketball. In reality, the following is how the summer actually played out…Rowan was very busy with track skills development over the summer while the weather was nice, along with raising steers for college money. Noah played on a traveling baseball team all summer. Tyler loved to farm and work; he also spent a lot of the summer in the mountains and on the lake. Cole's summer was filled with marksmanship since he was a high-level competitor in that sport. Dillon hadn't played basketball since junior high and spent his summers working on his family's farm.

Matt also worked long hours all summer helping with custom farming. Carter was tall and strong but carried a persistent knee injury that needed care and kept him out of the gym. Craig had never played a High School level sport. Sam, Klayton, Chris, and Jaskaran were all juniors and had their own summer distractions; they filled in the rest of the bench. None of them made it to summer basketball. All had limited varsity experience due to the previous year's team of 12 superstar seniors. Their fate seemed obvious, but could they change their stars?

> "I love it when other people doubt me.
> It makes me work harder to prove them wrong."

Derek Jeter, American former professional baseball shortstop, businessman, and baseball executive.

The Underdog

Rowan and Noah were chosen as team captains. Both good leaders with strong competitive natures. The truth is, each player was talented, gifted differently and they all got along well. Even so, not one thing pointed toward any grand expectations. Putting them together on the court caused a lack of harmony. The season forecasted bleak at best. Many sighed and commented on the unfortunate absence of skill. Some believed maybe it wasn't so much a lack of fundamentals as a lack of focus. Nonetheless, this was the consensus that rippled through Burns.

Rowan and Noah

Coach Peters and Coach Mitchell's demeanor often suggested their only wish was to survive the season. They were very invested in last year's team as they had all the qualities coaches look for in a team that could win a State Championship. The 2014 season's "Dream Team" left no time or vision to develop this year's group. The ball was handed to this new team with lackluster faith and that is likely how they received it.

"I've always been seen as the underdog in everything I've ever done in my life, and it doesn't bother me in the slightest.

The lessons have just made me stronger."

Victor Ortiz, American professional boxer and film actor

Underdog (n)

1. Nothing to lose

2. Everything to gain

Destiny

Not one player, coach, parent, or fan had a clue how this team would forever change so many hearts and minds in a single season. In fact, it seemed it would be the opposite. Would it be a season to remember? Or maybe forget?

It all started at a home tournament. The floor had been refinished over the summer; the gloss shined so strong it resembled a mirror. The smell of fresh varnish was a reminder of great plays and events of history the gym held. The scoreboard was bright with red lights and ready to announce the scores. The smell of popcorn and the color orange permeated the stands.

The band played with all the usual zest they always did as the tuba, trumpets, and drums helped build the excitement and anticipation of what would take place on that sparkly, magnificent floor. The gym was packed with parents, students, and friends as the sounds of a new basketball season filled the air. The announcer introduced the starters with enthusiasm and each one felt like a superstar for that moment. Rowan and Noah led with energy, strength, and their special ritual of jumps and fist bumps. It seemed everyone forgot about the predictions as the Broncs lined up for the tip-off. The starting buzzer, on that fateful day, set the team's destiny into motion.

"Destiny is all!"

Uhtred Ragnarson, a mighty warrior with high reputation from The Last Kingdom.

Written by Bernard Cornwell

The Team

This kick-off tournament proved to be a very rough start. Each player contributed in their own way and yet the team was discombobulated.

Rowan almost always won the jump ball and was able to move down the court with grace and lots of air. Noah was focused and competitive, willing to take the right risks to get points scored. Tyler was fast with no fear and a never-ending tough spirit. Cole stood tall and excelled at letting the other team run into him as he stood his ground; he could make a lot of shots.

Carter also shot well and contributed to the score when his teammates got the ball to him. Dylan was a defensive beast and a great dribbler. Matt was aggressive and quick. Craig filled in whenever needed and had a great attitude. Sam, Klayton, Chris, and Jas filled in with athletics and a special spirit of brotherhood.

But could these "12 Strong" find a way to gel together as a team? That was the riddle that needed to be solved.

Rowan #2

"To say my fate is not tied to your fate is like saying, 'Your end of the boat is sinking'"

Hugh Downs, American radio and television broadcaster

Courage

Despite what seemed to be a great mix of strengths, the endings were all losses. They struggled to play together mentally; with each game the more real the struggle appeared. It was as if they had been given a puzzle they couldn't solve, a mystery they couldn't find the answer to.

Noah #21

The year to remember unfolded as their bus took them every single week, many miles up and down the two-lane highways, to other water tower towns. Facing discouraging facts, including the standings, every game day the Broncs showed up! Ties, haircuts, and hope are what they had. Their warm-ups were impressive with an energy that caused wonder in the stands. With their arms around each other's shoulders in their huddle, they swayed back and forth, while the spaces between each player would make the shape of a heart. As the parents watched the hearts form from the stands their hearts ached for the team.

"Go down swinging. And I'll tell you: If you fight with all you have, more often than not, you won't go down at all. You will win"

Jocko Willink, Navy Seal, author, podcaster.

Fate

It just didn't seem like success was in the cards for them, no matter how hard they fought; or how much everyone prayed. Was learning to lose all that was in store for them? In the midst of their struggles, they had an unspoken bond that only a band of brothers do; like troops heading to war, knowing they were outnumbered, outgunned, and possibly going to come up short of a miracle...again! It was a sort of war, one they faced over and over, to keep their spirit alive and not lose it to discouragement; to be willing to fight for their teammates at all costs.

Tyler #1

The parents and fans watched each game with lumps in their throats and heavy hearts. They bonded as well, agreeing to pray and never give up on this seemingly ill-fated team. Secretly each parent might have wondered if the others were failing in their faith as the prayers seemed to remain unanswered.

Cole #52

"When brothers agree, no fortress is so strong as their common life."

Antisthenes, Greek philosopher and a pupil of Socrates.

Statistics

When the season wound down their record was 6-27. Their conference record was 1-7. Yes, this was a season to remember, or maybe try to forget.

Carter #50

It wasn't just their record that loomed in their heads; in most games, the opposing team had around 20 more points under their name than the Broncs. Another chink in their armor. Adding insult to injury, Carter fell to a knee injury early on in the season which moved him permanently to a manager position. Tyler lost his temper for a split second and was out for the middle part of the season due to a broken hand. No one dared to ask what else could go wrong. In spite of the suffocating air of defeat, the Broncs chose not to let it show on the court or lose their composure; this seemed a miracle of sorts. Meanwhile, more and more people gave up on them.

Dylan #55

"Success is falling down nine times and getting up ten."

Jon Bon Jovi, one of America's most famous singers, songwriters, guitarist, and rock band star.

The Forecast

Even those who love long shots, comebacks, and underdogs never predicted what happened next.

At the end of the regular season, a traditional game called the pigtail game is played between the two last-place teams. The winner advances to the regional playoffs. As the last-place team, the Broncs received the bottom spot in that game. This also made it an away game. Some thought just getting it over with was best. This game seemed the ending place.

Matt #3

Even with the facts, the history, and the team's record, a miracle happened; or maybe just plain old grit grew like a snowdrift does in that windy town of Burns. They won! Only the second conference win of the season! A few hours earlier the trip to regionals had been a farfetched idea and yet…how did it happen? Was a culture forming on the team? Were they aware of it? Questions to be answered later in the story.

"The hardest skill to acquire in sports is the one where you compete all out, give it all you have, and you are still getting beat no matter what you do. When you have the killer instinct to fight through that, it is very special."

Eddie Reese, Olympic and American College Swimming Coach and former college swimmer.

The Odds

Getting ready for the Regional Tournament created excitement and fun and their seed of faith appeared to grow. The first game of the tournament proved tough; they played well but got edged out by a very good team. Now it was win, or go home! Game two started worse than bad…at halftime, the score showed the Broncs down by 22 points.

Craig #22

It is a mystery to this day what happened in the locker room during halftime. Shock and awe are what happened in the gym during the second half of that game as they climbed back from so far down it had to be seen to be believed. It had all the feels of a miracle. Most just watched in wonder. This win would take them to another game; another chance or another miracle; whichever you choose to believe.

Sam #33

"Odds and rankings don't matter. This is the theory of fighting and not math. I just believe in myself and go out and do it."

Mike Chiesa, American professional mixed martial artist, and sports analyst.

The Fight

The next game would determine their fate for the state tournament. The schedule put them against a rival that had beat them significantly several times. Before the game, the mother of one of the opposing team's players commented, "We are definitely going to state! The Broncs are so easy to beat!" She had obviously failed to notice the character that had been growing in the Broncs, a team willing to persevere against all odds! Unbeknownst even to themselves, they had been growing fortitude and resolve like zucchini in a summer garden.

Klayton #32

You could have heard a pin drop as the whistle blew to start the game; what would happen now? Were they out of comebacks and miracles?

The bond between parents was also strong as they stood like a wall in the stands and in rare comradery. The grit the Broncs displayed was impossible to watch without getting a lump in your throat. The other team sensed it and it became too powerful for them to overcome. Tears rolled as the Broncs ran away with that win! One that washed away much of the pain and agony from the brutal season and losses suffered. Enough criticism to make even the toughest warriors quit.

Chris #23

"It's not the size of the dog in the fight, it's the size of the fight in the dog."

Mark Twain, American writer, humorist, entrepreneur, and publisher.

Resolve

The quiet disbelief from the opposing side did not go unnoticed as they suffered a huge loss from the last place team, knocking them out of the State Tournament. The opposing coach was so shocked he threw his clipboard in 2-year-old tantrum fashion. I am sure they wondered how this happened, but only the Broncs knew the answer to that question.

Jas #44

After that game, a radio broadcaster shared how he watched the Broncs at breakfast that morning. He explained the way they carried themselves was something to witness. Arriving at breakfast in ties and game faces; there was no messing around. Resolve filled the air. It was almost suffocating. He said, "It was a powerful moment that made me take note, eager to see them play." None of it was planned or discussed; it only had to do with who they had become, Champions of Character.

"Moral courage is the most valuable and usually the most absent characteristic among men."

George S Patton, United States Army General, Commander of the Seventh Army in World War II.

Grit

With the bus decorated, the team received a grand send-off to the state tournament.

"We are a team that almost didn't even make it to regionals, and now we're playing at state. We have nothing left to prove," said Rowan, "We're not going up there scared that we're going to get knocked off our pedestal. We are just going to go play basketball as hard as we can and the best we can."

The first game was a tough loss against the number one seed. They played tough but were outnumbered, outsized, and outcoached. Would it smash their faith? It was a strong possibility as they learned their next game was against a team that had eliminated many former Broncs teams over the years from the State Tournament.

After everything that had happened was there more in store for this team? The anticipation was suffocating. Not one person left the stands or sat down during game two of the State Tournament. The score flew back and forth like a windshield wiper on high! Watching that game was like trying to see the road between wipes of the blades and the downpour as it covers your windshield. Like white-knuckle driving, it was all a blur!

"Never, never, never give in!"

Winston S. Churchill, a British statesman who served as Prime Minister of the United Kingdom from 1940 to 1945, during the Second World War, and again from 1951 to 1955.

Gifted

When the end game buzzer rang the board showed 46-43! Broncs win! Without a doubt the best game of the season!

Rowan spoke, "We kept working hard and didn't quit. We just kept going after it and got the feeling that Lusk was quitting before the game was over."

This may have been the mountaintop moment of the entire season. Many wondered how the Broncs recognized their opponent's will beginning to weaken. Did the answer have to do with the fact that fighting to the end was the only way the Broncs knew how to play? Or was it that the Bronc's opponents had never learned how to pull up their killer instinct to finish a battle? The Broncs used their endless losses to bond them together. They learned to scrap and persist until the last buzzer rang. Their opponents did not earn the gifts these scars provide.

"There is generosity in our scars."

Scott Mann, Us Army Green Beret. Army Special Forces Career in Foreign Internal Defense, Counter-insurgency, and Stability Missions all over the world.

The Legacy

Is it possible that hardships sometimes offer the greatest gifts of all? That fighting through obstacles offers more than luck and natural talent ever can?

Many hearts were changed that season and what a beautiful gift it was.

Whatever life could throw at these players after this was bound to be met with the same character they used throughout the worst/best season the Broncs ever had. Executing the greatest comeback season in the history of Burns Broncs Basketball is the legacy of grit they left for others to follow. Proof of what the faith of a mustard seed can do. And confirmation that a fight to the end is always the right answer.

"Most people give up just when they're about to achieve success. They quit on the one-yard line. They give up at the last minute of the game one foot from a winning touchdown."

Ross Perot, American business magnate, billionaire, politician, and philanthropist.

The Champions

In the end, it wasn't about how they placed. Their never-give-up spirit won them fourth at the State Tournament but most importantly, the trophy and title of a lifetime, "Champions of Character." Grit always wins over talent!

Grit…passion and perseverance in pursuit of long-term goals. Grit determines who is tough enough not to be a quitter.

Family and Fans

Parents and forever fans of the Broncos 2015

Rowan and Dad

Noah and Dad

"You have to do something in your life that is honorable and not cowardly if you are to live at peace with yourself'

Larry Brown, American Basketball Coach, former player, and the only coach to win both an NCAA and NBA Championship.

Moms of the Team

Seniors and Parents

www.ingramcontent.com/pod-product-compliance
Lightning Source LLC
Chambersburg PA
CBHW040720170426
43209CB00046B/1718